Workbook Nine

Of the Business Essentials

Series

GETTING BACK

YOUR TIME

John Millar

ISBN:1537432818
ISBN-13:9781537432816

DEDICATION

I dedicate this book to my mother and father, who raised me while self-employed. They taught me to work hard and listen to everyone but to make my own choices as to what is right and what is wrong.. and oh, did I mention work hard?

Anyone who tells you to work smart not hard hasn't ever done it tough and realized that if you work smart AND hard you will achieve more than you can possibly dream.

CONTENTS

PRODUCT DESCRIPTION

Time management is an essential skill for successful progress in all walks of life. We choose how we utilise our time. We can either allow time to control our activities or we can make time work for us by establishing priorities and schedules. Effective time management is about getting more done with your available time.

Effective time management involves learning a number of vital skills.

1. Goal setting – knowing what you are trying to achieve. This helps you to stay motivated and manage your time more effectively. To set goals, you need to decide on your long term, medium term and short term goals. The time frames will vary for each individual but future success and development will be seriously jeopardised without setting your goals.

2. Prioritising and getting the most done in the most efficient and effective way. Time is limited and valuable, so it must be allocated wisely. Discover where you lose precious time and how you can recover it to work better for you.

3. Planning your time. This means planning ahead and taking control of your time. Planning regularly allows you to achieve your goals, monitor your progress and prevent time wastage. It also means you can eliminate a lot of wasted interruptions by having timed sessions allocated to specific tasks.

4. Making the best use of your time. Time is a valuable resource that should be put to good use.

This is where you get to redefine your time management and reclaim ownership of your schedule.

You will better understand how you can work more on your business than in it and see a clearer picture of your business and its progress

You will also finally find out why others can seem to fit more into their day while having a great LIFE – WORK balance (notice the order!)..

Regards,

John Millar

Today's topic has more about self-management and organization than what you will traditionally apply to principles of time management. Are you applying good self-management and organization skills and tools? Are you doing the most productive thing that you can do at every moment of the day or simply on cruise control bumping around?

Take the challenge and apply discipline to what I will show you and your quality of life and the quality of your business can't do anything but improve.

It's often not what you know; it's what you do with what you know! How much do you know about good time management, self-management and organization and just don't do anything with that knowledge?

What can you do inside your business to make sure you get your half and half right? Where your half is your distribution and the other half is the marketing. Because there's no use marketing and promising something that you can't deliver.

1. ....

2. ....

3. ....

4. ....

5. ....

Remember information without application is an obscenity.

Are you busy being busy or are you busy being productive?

Time is your number one asset. It's a non-renewable resource that's so precious and valuable and yet we see people time and time again who will spend time to save money rather than investing money to save time. Truly successful people more often invest money to save time because they know they can make more money but you simply can't make more time.

We need to be able to convert your knowledge, your genius, and your efforts through the investment of time into money.

How do we go about doing that?

First of all I believe establishing a base earning target that you want to earn as an individual and as a business owner. You need to actually look at how many hours that you will genuinely be productive in each and every day and which of those hours directly generate revenue for you and your business.

How much are you worth to yourself and to your business every hour of the day?

....
....
....

What are the activities and tasks that are simply sucking up your time and are consuming your time and resources and that are not allowing you while you're in your business to generate more revenue?

1. ....

2. ....

3. ....

4. ....

5. ....

6. ....

7 ....

8. ....

9 ....

GETTING BACK YOUR TIME

10

> What are you currently doing in your business that is probably better done by someone else inside your business or you can outsource to someone who will do it faster and better and allow you to focus on income generating activities?

1.

2.

3.

4.

5.

6.

7

8.

9

10

You're the most valuable person in the business and yet most business owners don't value their own time!

How much time you're actually spending commuting, paperwork, filing, book keeping, answering the phone, basic facile things within the business that you could engage somebody else to do and free your time up for more proactive and productive revenue and profit generating activities?

1. ....

2. ....

3. ....

4. ....

5. ....

6. ....

7 ....

8. ....

9 ....

10 ....

....

Once you then put a meter on the consumption of your time, you then need to actually quantify what's actually going on inside your life.

....

....

....

....

How many billable hours are you actually working in your business?

....

....

Within time mastery there are three major sectors.

The first of all, the most important of all and the one that everybody seems to want to escape from is self-mastery. You need to be able to master yourself. What is self-mastery to you?

1. ....

2. ....

3. ....

4. ....

5. ....

The second is the ability to implement quality planning within your business. How much planning have you done and what do you still need to do?

1. ....

2. ....

3. ....

4. ....

5. ....

Finally and very importantly is the art of delegation. How much do you delegate and do you delegate well?

1.

2.

3.

4.

5.

There is no such thing as time management. It's all about self-management!
Unless you have some secret power to bend time and space?

Do you manage your time or are you allowing it to be managed for you?

You need to start looking at managing things and preparing before they occur rather than just putting out fires and running between crisis.

You must make sure that you've applied discipline internally and externally.

Most business owners need an external pressure or external assistance to help them with their internal discipline and that's okay.

How do you bring that pressure and assistance in your business?

1. ....

2. ....

3. ....

4. ....

5. ....

Make sure that external pressure creates internal discipline

You must look at every self-development opportunity that you have. So, whether that be attending a workshop, a seminar, a personal development program, reading a book, listening to an audio. There's a whole host of things that you can actually do to improve yourself. List 10 things you are going to do to improve yourself personally and professionally over the next 90 days.

1. ....

2. ....

3. ....

4. ....

5. ....

6. ....

7

8.

9

10

For things to change, first I must change

What do you need to change for things to change?

1.

2.

3.

4.

5.

6.

7

8.

9

10

It's about self-management first and foremost

The definition of insanity is continuing to do the same thing we've always done and expecting a different outcome.

You must look at things in regards to urgency versus importance

1. Not Urgent and Not Important. (Distraction)

What tasks are you doing on a day-to-day basis that fall into this category? Surfing the net, sending funny emails, reading the paper, getting the milk? This is the category of trivia, gossip and time wasting.

2. Urgent and Not Important. (Delusion)

This is where business owners regularly get caught, constantly answering other people's questions and doing their tasks and jobs. Yes, they are Urgent but are they Important? In most cases NO! Some meetings, some calls and interruptions will fall into this category. A good example of this is the tradesman that does a quote knowing very well that they are never going to get the job.

3. Urgent and Important. (Demand)

This is the category in which many business owners spend the majority of their time. It includes the day to day tasks in a business such as dealing with customers, suppliers and staff.

4. Not Urgent and Important. (Zone)

These tasks don't have any urgency but they are important. This is the easiest category to avoid simply because it doesn't have any urgency. This is where the Entrepreneur/Strategist needs to live!
Here is where all those things that you know you need to do are, but you just haven't got around to doing them yet. Tasks in this category include documenting a business plan, marketing, planning and training your team. This will also include family time, relationship time, fitness and health—how much time are you devoting to this?

So, in other words and you had used this example before. Standing here today, is my health important? Yes, but its urgent no, but if I killed over with a heart attack, is my health important? Yes, it still remains important but what's changed is the urgency that's changed. So, don't wait until you have a veritable heart attack within your business. Make sure that you work at your urgency versus important and make sure you focus on the most urgent and most important things in your life and in your business every single day.

At the end of every day, you should sit down and work at the list of tasks that you're going to undertake tomorrow, the goals, the outcomes that you're looking to achieve every single day and this is a process, you must cover at the end of every day.

You got to take that list and break it down to A, B, C priorities. Now, my attitudes are well A has to be done; it's the most important thing. It's not negotiable. The B stands for I'll be doing it when I'll finish the A's and the C stands for well I'll see what I can do when I finish the Bs. Now, if you haven't broken things down to a priority, what happens, we usually end up being sucked into the activities that are very urgent but not necessarily important or if they are important, not necessarily important to you. You've got to use your goals to focus those things because if those things that you're planning to undertake are not stepping you one step closer to your goal then why you're doing it, eliminate it, stop making excuses and just stop it. This is when we're talking about self-knowledge and self-capacity for self-management.

So, again do the As first then the Bs when you have time and the Cs are to delegate them to someone else or if you can't delegate it to somebody else, see what you can do when you finish the Bs.

Look at some of the tasks that you do regularly and routinely and write them in A, B, or C.

Task	Frequency	Priority

I'm sure that you came up with more than two or three things that you do every day which fall really into the C category and the things that fall into the A&B Category.

> If you are not allocating at least an hour a day to work on your business you have wasted your day. This could be self-development training, it could be reading a book, it could be your business planning, a whole host of different things. If you are not doing those things then you are wasting significant opportunities to be able to grow and develop your business.

Do you own a business or have you bought yourself a job?

JUST
OVER
BROKE

Have you taken your business to where you dreamed it should be when you first started? What did you see for your business when you started?

1. ....

2.   · ....

3. ....

4. ....

5. ....

6. ....

7 ....

8. ....

9 ....

10 ....

I'm sure you didn't start this business expecting to work the most amounts of hours and earn the least amount yet this is what we see commonly happening within most businesses.

I want to undertake a time block study throughout your day.

Daily Time Record Sheet   Name:_____ Date: ___/___/_____

From	To	Activity	Position / Task
:00	:20		
:20	:40		
:40	:00		
:00	:20		
:20	:40		
:40	:00		
:00	:20		
:20	:40		
:40	:00		
:00	:20		
:20	:40		
:40	:00		
:00	:20		
:20	:40		
:40	:00		
:00	:20		
:20	:40		
:40	:00		
:00	:20		
:20	:40		
:40	:00		
:00	:20		
:20	:40		
:40	:00		

Instructions for Daily Time Record Sheet

1. Use one sheet entitled, "Daily Time Record Sheet" for each day. Enter your Name, Day of the week and the Date at the top of the page, where indicated.
    Example: Name : Bill Smith Date : Tue, 23 Feb 2009.

2. In the columns labelled, "From" and "To", note the time your work day begins. Example: 7:00 to 7:20. You should have adequate space to log your day in twenty (20) minute time blocks running down the page.

3. Beside each twenty (20) minute block (in the column entitled "Activity"), write a brief description of the major activity that took place. If more than one significant activity took place, split the space with a diagonal line and enter both. Be as specific about what you did as possible. A sample is shown below:

    1:00 1:20 Sales meeting
    1:20 1:40 Sales meeting
    1:40 2:00 Reviewed accounts / called FB to make an appointment

4. In the column titled Position/Task detail the position on the Organizational chart responsible and a description of the job task. (e.g. Sales - Quoting, Prod Plan - Ordering, Admin - Get Mail, etc)

5. Make each entry as soon after completion of the activity as is feasible. Immediacy reduces forgetting events, mixing up facts or under-overstating the time certain activities actually took to complete.

6. Keep in mind that the time invested in recording on these time logs (approximately 15 minutes spread out over each day) will be more than recovered when you see the results of your analysis and find opportunities to make better use of your time.

7. Plan to log your time use for at least three (3) full work days. The data you collect should be "representative" of how you spend your time. Do not be concerned about which days you select to log your activities. In our business, there is no such thing as a "typical" or "normal" day, is there?

> Now, let me forewarn you, this is painful but worth the 15 minutes a day it takes to do.

....
....
....
....

You need to actually determine within that 20 minute increment what you actually do for that day, what you did during that time period, what was the thing that took out most of that time and how much value did you offer your business.

....
....
....
....

My challenge to you is to make sure that you go through and do this time block study and make sure that you use this information to set up your default diary.

....
....
....
....

Any activity that occurs within your day that cost less to actually get someone else to do it than what your worth is to the business, I would suggest you go and get someone else to do it. What should you let go of?

1. ....

2. ....

3. ....

4. ....

5. ....

6. ....

7. ....

8. ....

9. ....

10. ....

Remember truly successful people will invest money to save time and unsuccessful people usually spend time to save money.

Set up your default diary

	Monday	Tuesday	Wednesday	Thursday	Friday
6:00 AM					
7:00 AM	IVVM-AFFIRMATIONS	IVVM-AFFIRMATIONS	IVVM-AFFIRMATIONS	IVVM-AFFIRMATIONS	NJAZ Team Call
8:00 AM	AZ Team Call	COLD CALLS	COLD CALLS	COLD CALLS	COLD CALLS
9:00 AM	Gateway	COLD CALLS	Return/FU Calls prospects/Mailing	COLD CALLS	COLD CALLS
10:00 AM	Direct Mail to Seminar attendees	90-Day Plan	Clean/Create Documents/Systems	Group Coaching	Gateway
11:00 AM			COLD CALLS		FORUM
12:00 PM	Role Play Cell	LUNCH	BNI	LUNCH	Toastmasters
01:00 PM	Client Prep	Return/FU Calls prospects/Mailing	Practice Seminar	90-Day Plan	Coffee News Coaching
02:00 PM	Quarterly Articles	Clean/Create Documents/ Systems		Database management	OFF
03:00 PM	FORUM				OFF
04:00 PM	Education/ Reading	Education/ Reading	Gateway	TOM COACHING	OFF
05:00 PM	PLAN FOR TOMORROW	PLAN FOR TOMORROW	PLAN FOR TOMORROW	PLAN FOR TOMORROW	PLAN FOR TOMORROW
06:00 PM	EXERCISE	EXERCISE	EXERCISE	EXERCISE	EXERCISE

Calculate your base earning worth

Base Earnings: $_____

Divided by 1760 hours (220 days x 8 = 1760 work hours in a year)

    = base hourly rate $_____

    X % of time spent productively

    vs. non-productively   _____

    = What your time must be

    worth per hour : $_____

Why do so many business owners go through all the risk of working inside your business when your base area rate is so low and you can make more money working for someone else without the stress?

Our whole goal is to be working the least amount of hours and earning the most amount of

Look at what you actually do to be productive throughout the day and what percentage of time that was non-productive.

....

....

....

Have a look at our ABCs in your clients whether they are internal and external costumer. This could be team members or this could be supplies or et cetera or this could be actual customers who purchase their goods and services. If we break them down and we look at them into A for awesome, these are the ones that we want to treat like royalty and family. Now B is their basic customer, they're what we expect as a very minimum based on to their business with this. The C is we can't do with and we want to get rid of them and then D is the dead.

....

....

....

How many of the people on your database do you actually interact with? how often and is it in a meaningful manner?

....

....

....

....

....

....

....

....

....

....

....

....

....

Make sure you clean up your database if you haven't got one, get one and make sure that it's up to date and clean. Get rid of those dead ones out there because again stop killing yourself. Get rid of the can't deal with, introduce them to your greatest competitor and let them deal with the pains in the neck that are usually costing your money. Who are you doing business with that you shouldn't be?

1.

2.

3.

4.

5.

6.

7.

8.

9.

10.

Any good plan is a simple plan.

Keep it simple stupid.

It needs to have some action.

It needs to have momentum and movement

The next part of a plan is it must be based upon what you are or going to do not just a theory behind it.

Develop a to do or what needs to be done when we're taking our plan into effect

Sales is the only thing that brings revenue into your business and it's one area where most people in the business neglect Theory behind it.

So often I see sales people who have been devalued by the business owners.

Look at the value of an opportunity and make sure it's a real opportunity and not just a WOFTAM.

A WOFTOM is a Waste Of Flipping Time And Money.

They're people that you would, could, should, maybe, I see it so often in the building and trade and manufacturing industries where they do a quote in their full knowledge that they're probably not even going to get the business but you know what if I keep wasting my time and I keep investing my money so that they can cross quote with the person I will going to buy from anyway then maybe I'm going to win the business.

Stop kidding yourself. Stop wasting your most valuable resource which is your time. Stop just deluding yourself. Send them to somebody else who you would rather see their time, money, energy, resources and tools wasted rather than wasting yours.

When we're actually building a plan, developing a plan, we go to build the plan and then work the plan. Just because we built the plan in the first place doesn't necessarily mean it's going to stay hard and fast, business is a growing, adopting, organisms. So, that plan really needs to be worked.

In the first instance to put it down on paper.

Make sure that you invested allocated the time to think.

Make sure that you've got your default diary set up to give you the time to implement your plans and strategies.

If you don't allocate time to get things done then it will take as long as you allow it to

Ensure that you have taken disciplines to remove delusion and distraction as much from your day as possible.

What are the things that you can actually do and what do you need to do to remove delusions and distractions?

1. _____

2. _____

3. _____

4. _____

5. _____

6. _____

7. _____

8. _____

9. _____

10. _____

Look at your art of delegation.

Most business owners are strong, upright driven people. Unfortunately, most of them are also control freaks.

Once you've done that basic time log, you look for those tasks that should be delegated not just can be but should be delegated and remember they are usually tasks that are worth less to the business than what you can generate for the business.

What are the basic things that you can delegate straight away?

1.

2.

3.

4.

5.

6.

7.

8.

9.

10.

What is it that you wouldn't be able to delegate today but want to within the next 90 days?

1. ....

2. ....

3. ....

4. ....

5. ....

6. ....

7. ....

8. ....

9. ....

10. ....
....

So, why are you wasting your time?

....

....

....

Make sure you train, assist, mentor your team and measure the progress of everything that you delegate otherwise it's not delegation its abdication.

....
....
....

What do you want to be able to delegate within the next 12 months?

1. ....

2. ....

3. ....

4. ....

5. ....

6. ....

7. ....

8. ....

9. ....

10. ....

Are you controlling your business or is your business controlling you?

....
....
....

There's only four areas to able to leverage these things within the business.

The first and foremost is the people, the team that we have

The second is the education that we provide ourselves and how provide to our team.

Third it's the systems that we created, developed and implemented within the business and the technology that we can actually use to make sure that those systems work well and consistently.

The fourth is delivery and distribution and making sure that they are consistent and that we are delivering and distributing the right things at the right time and that at all times that we constantly testing and measuring.

What are we doing and test and measure so we can celebrate our wins?

You need to make two business life changes.

The first and foremost is you must surround yourself with people that have respect for you and value your time and behave accordingly.

The second business life change that I believe make such a significant change in things is for you to eliminate the need for doing or delegate those task or activities that just cannot or do not match up with the mandated value of your time.

You need to build your and your team's productivity. You need to be able to create urgency and timeliness in everything that you do, making sure that we set ourselves high priority tasks and we delegate the lower priority tasks other to another person or to another day.

Are you making sure everything's done in full on time?

Do you systemize the routine and humanize the exceptions?

Do you encourage and support risk taking?

Unfortunately many of us are caught up with our business for so long that we spent 20% of our time systemizing the routine and 80% trying to humanize it. It does not work that way because now we don't have a consistent steady business that we know that we can count upon.

Beware the following people in your business

Time vampires

These are the ones that consistently texting you rather than picking up the phone and calling you ONCE. They send you joke emails or again have conversations via email rather than picking up the phone or seeing you face to face. They drop by without notice and say hey look you got a minute and then take an hour?

They fail to understand that Text and emails are great for TELLING people things but not great for conversations. They are also phone hogs so if they do ring you rather than cover everything in one call they will ring you multiple times.

This is completely unplanned by them so the only way that you can moderate the have you got a minute time vampires is to actually invite them to go over specific things at specific times with "look I'm sorry but I'm really busy at the moment but let's catch up between 3:30 and 3:45 and we'll go over those things unless they're incredibly urgent and can't wait until then".

Mr. Meeting.

You've got those people who have got nothing better to do than actually attend meetings and these are people who often get caught up in decision making by committee. They need to stop and evaluate and get everything to 110%. They just want to have a meeting on something, on anything, on everything. Often times a meeting is a good idea but frequently that is not necessarily the case and there are more effective ways to be able to handle it.

If you do need to have a meeting with these Mr. Meetings you MUST have an agenda, Discuss beforehand what needs to be achieved in the meeting and what activities and outcomes and actions are going to be the result. How often have you heard the same, "oh we keep meeting all the time but nothing ever seems to come out of it." You must manage this or you will spend all your time in meetings and never actually get things done. The government has this down to a fine art and we all know how inefficient they can be and how long it can take to get a decision and action.

Mr. Trivia.

Mr. Trivia is the person who just can't differentiate between what's important what's unimportant, what's minor, what's major, what's urgent, what's not urgent and you really need to get them to understand what's really important and just eliminate the trivia. Let them know that you're only dealing with what they want to give to you if you're going to put on a scale of 1 to 10. You need to deal with 9s and 10s and there might be somebody else better suited to deal with the 8 and below. Just because it's important to them doesn't make it important to you and your business

Emotional Vampire

These are the people who make mountains out of mall hills. These are the people who are never so happy as when they're miserable. Everything is always blowing right out of proportion. What you need to do with them is I'm sorry but to be cruel to be kind is just to the cut to the core of problem and give them a solution, cut them short, there is times and places that you need to be able to share those things emotionally and personally together but people who will run on emotional crisis to emotional crisis to emotional crisis that's not the way to go, if you are that person and think about the plan and what you can do to actually stop that.

Time vampires will only succeed if you let them

It's your responsibility if you buy into their activity.

Take a few minutes, think now about your time vampires that are either you or people around allow and what you can actually do each day to make sure that they don't suck the lifeblood out of your business.

What time vampires are you dealing with and are you one of those vampires?

Time vampires are prevalent and you know what they hang around during the daytime not just night time.

What do I want and what do I expect from others and what do I others expect from me. What should they expect? How tough are you on those who actually under value your time?

Some interruption strategies to help kill time vampires

Get lost, in other words be inaccessible, close the door and don't let things interrupt you

....

....

....

....

....

Don't answer the phone, have a receptionist, voice mail or something else act as a buffer between you.

....

....

....

....

Create that steel curtain of defense in between you and those things that try so hard to interrupt you.

....

....

....

....

....

When you check your emails check those things that you take care of the urgent things first and the least urgent things second. Emails are classic because they are great way to be able to communicate great business information but I ask people again to send me a joke or an interesting email that's not business related to send it to my home email address. Now, I check my business email address twice a day but I check my home email address maybe once or twice a week. So, that way the things that are interesting but not relevant to my business are not going to interrupt my day.

Make sure that you're visibly busy to other people.

....

....

....

....

....

Have some honest, self-analysis and self-understanding about what your specialties are, what is it that you do extraordinarily well within the business, because when you're aware of that then you can understand the next stage which is what you need to delegate.

....

....

....

....

When you look into delegate these are series of steps

First of all you need to do to find what is to be done

....

....

....

....

The second thing is find the right person to delegate to and to be certain the person that you delegated to actually understands what needs to be done.

....

....

....

....

....

Remember there are only 3 reasons why people don't do things in this world. One of which is they don't understand what you ask them to do, you ask them to do too much or they didn't understand the relevance or importance as to why they need to do it, what the outcome positive and negative is going to be if they don't.

Thirdly make absolutely certain that the person understands the how to of the process so they really know how to do those things. You need to make sure that when you delegate that you set a deadline or completion date to make sure that they report their progress along the way and then making sure that you got agreement on the date and the time that something's going to be absolutely finalized on.

Welcome your own dispensability, understand that you're maybe good at what you do but you know what there's probably somebody out there better at a particular task.

Too often business owners make themselves indispensable because they feel safer.

When you have a task and you haven't written it down, you're actually destined to repeat it again and again.

Twelve time management techniques that are worth using every single day.

First and foremost, tame the phone, fax and email

Second of all, make sure that you minimize the meetings that you have, maximize the outcomes.

Third, make sure that others value your time as much as you do.

Fourth, make use of list and schedules and to do list,

Fifth, link everything to your goals

Sixth, look at tickle files

Seventh, make sure that you block out your time and default diary your time

Eighth, minimize all unplanned activities during planned work hours

Ninth, make sure that you have broken your day down in 30 minute blocks.

Tenth focus less on time management and put more into energy management

Eleventh, profit from the times which are usually down times.

Twelfth , live off peak.

I promise you that if you do get yourself and therefore your time under control, the quality of your life, the quality of your business, the output and the energy that you can sustain will be far greater than you've ever achieve before.

John Millar

Additional information to read:

BASIC PREMISES

- **Accept** – you will never be able to do everything you want… because there is just too much to do.
- **Purpose** - the driving force behind managing your time is to accomplish your ultimate goal/s.

FOUR SKILLS required to use your time

- Analysis
- Planning
- Delegation
- Self-management

THE PROCESS for success

- What to do:
- Spend your time doing what is key to the success of your business
- Work on tasks that can only be done effectively by you.
- (4 "D's" -- Do it…. Delegate it….Defer it….or Dump it)

- When to do
- Plan your time/ organise your work schedule so that you are never working the issues that fall into the two "Not Important" categories.

- How to do (organise)
- Create a "template" schedule for each time period – month/week/day - which allocates time periods for specific types of tasks. Ex: travel to customers, return/place phone calls; do quiet work, organize paperwork, read.
- Tool – Time blocking chart

- How to do (discipline)
- The key to efficient use of time is planning
- Work from lists & mark the items for priority (a,b,c) -

- Tool – Daily, Weekly lists

PLANNING

- **For efficiency**
- Do it in advance -- Friday night or weekend for next week; the night before, for the next day, rather than the morning of.
-Gather your materials in advance, so can "hit the ground running"

- **For motivation**
- Put as much on your list as you can, momentum gained as you check off
- When large projects, break them into small steps so you can see progress.

- **For effectiveness**
- Each major project should be planned out over time periods - with other activities interspersed

HINTS for SUCCESS

- Incremental progress is key. So for projects, "divide to multiply".

- Start now, step by step.

- Do the toughest things first.
- stops procrastination
- you'll feel great... therefore...
- you'll be inspired to do everything else required for the day

- Delegate.
- Include scheduled time in your plan to oversee/ train/ obtain & review reports on the work you have delegated.
- Do not slip into the habit of doing it.

IF YOU SCHEDULE ON IMPORTANCE NOT URGENCY –
THE URGENT WILL ALMOST NEVER OCCUR!

Are you driving your business or is your business driving you?

Growing a business can be challenging, but a clear strategy and a set of systems can help take the pain out of growth.

There comes a point in most small businesses when the owner – you – stands back and acknowledges that it can no longer be classed as a start-up and that it's time for it to grow to the next stage.

The challenge now is how do you do that? More of the same? Probably not.

You've done a great job to get to where you are now, but to get to the next stage will need a bigger plan.

Develop your vision

What do you want your business to become? How will it behave? What will set it apart from its competition? Decide what your growth goals are and set yourself targets and set some realistic milestones by which you can measure your progress.

These will include your revenue targets, the timeframe in which you will achieve this, number of staff and when they will join the business, number of outlets, profitability and so on.

The key is to map out a growth destination that is real, but stretches you and that can be broken down into smaller goals. Planning growth in your business also needs you to work on developing yourself as a manager and a leader. Be prepared to get out of your comfort zone and grow as a person as your business will be a reflection of you.

Your next task is to be really objective and honest about the business as it is now. If it has just come out of start-up stage then it is almost certainly still very 'you-dependent'.

In other words, without you there it would not be able to operate effectively, let alone grow. This is a wake-up moment, and a very valuable realisation, because you are now able to ask yourself key questions about what really needs to be in place for growth to happen.

Time for action

The first thing is going to be time; specifically yours. Without you dedicating your time to business development, nothing will change. You are going to have to create some time in your working week.

Begin by identifying everything you do in a day, a week, a month. Work out which tasks you can delegate. (And if there is no one to delegate it to, you may have to consider getting in some office support – even if it's only a day or two a week.)

Introduce systems

Work out the instructions for each of the activities this person or people will be doing.

Imagine that they are doing the work without you there to tell them what comes next and set it all out on paper. These instructions must include clear steps, standards and timing. This is a system.
Make sure each system is recognisable as such and follows the same format.

Aim to free up at least one hour of your time every day – and when you have done that, begin to work on your growth plans and the systems that will streamline the work that needs to be done.

If you were to use that time just to develop one system, at the end of the week you would have five systems; at the end of the month, 20 and so on.

Key areas of focus

Incorporate into your planning the key areas your business will need to cover to ensure that the growth will be steady, managed and sustained.

Once you have a plan and created your thinking and development time, look at what your business will need in order to grow. If the answer is more sales, then maybe you should be looking at your marketing strategy.

If you have enough enquiries but are not converting them to business, then examine what is happening in your conversion process. Are you confident that your customer service department can deliver your products and services faultlessly and seamlessly? If not, then start there. Iron out the glitches. There is absolutely no point in developing a marketing strategy to bring in more business unless you know your business can deliver on its promises.

Think of your business as having four key strategic areas: production, marketing, management and resources. Then break those areas down into key areas. To begin with, you are going to be responsible for developing the strategies in all of these areas.

Systems for growth

Recognising that you need to implement systems is an important breakthrough. But before you can do that you need to 'systemise' yourself and your own thinking. Without that how could you possibly expect your staff to understand and adopt the same principles? In the beginning the systems that make the most difference will be deceptively simple and small ones."

It is through those systems that many of the daily frustrations and obstacles that prevent things running smoothly are eliminated. Gradually incorporate all the systems and guidelines into a handbook. Now everyone knows what to do and where they stand.

One of the most effective systems you can put in place was what I call your Exception Report. As most of the work we ask people to do is timeline-based we need to know if they can't complete something by a given time as this affects other team members. This will make everyone more aware of how their work impacts on others.

Anyone wanting to grow their business must know their target market. Really understand who they are, where they are and what motivates them. And, document everything and anything you do. Do not underestimate the importance of systems. This means that as people come into the business they know how things are done and there is a clear road map to follow.

Tips for growth planning

John Millar's tips for growth planning:

- Look for opportunities outside the norm that will still fit into your business framework
- Develop your staff and yourself
- Be committed and prepared to do what it takes
- Lead by example
- Plan for everything
- Systemize your business
- Put the right support structures in place
- Employ those who complement your skills
- Be prepared to turn away the wrong clients
- Find good advisers (legal, etc.)
- Develop a handbook for your policies and procedures.

John Millar's extra tips for growth planning:

- Get a business coach today if not sooner
- Define all the roles in the business
- Constantly review your strategic objective to keep on track
- Develop systems for everything and never underestimate their value
- See frustrations and complaints as opportunities to make your business better
- Delegate wherever you can
- Care for and develop your people
- Really know your target market
- Measure everything.

11 Most Important Tasks of Managers

Managing is one of the most important tasks in every business. Sometimes entrepreneurs are in the same time managers. There are plenty of tasks that managers must implement in everyday work activities that must bring effectiveness and efficiency in the business or organizational life. Here is one list of most important tasks of managers.

1. Coaching

One of the most important tasks of managers is coaching. They must be routers of the people in the business that will be routed through right instructions and training. The goal is to develop business with great business potential energy in their employees.

2. Planning

Planning is one of the management function and also one important everyday task of managers. They plan future ways where the business will go and activities that must be accomplished from organizational members.

3. Changing

In reality, there is not one day in business life without change. Change needs to be planned and managed to bring desired results. Managers in the same time must preserve the current success of the business and to implement change that will bring future success.

4. Forecasting

Forecasting is another task of managers that mean providing a picture of how will look like the business in the future. This is important because if we have the better picture for the future, we will be better prepared for that future.

5. Motivating

Peoples must be motivated to give the best results from their work. Nobody works for nothing. All employees have some type of motivational factors that will lead him to make better results. But, these motivational factors are different for each employee. Managerial tasks are to optimize that motivation and to maximize the working performances from employees. Motivating is another managerial function in addition to planning.

6. Organizing

Organizing is one of the managerial functions in addition to planning and motivating. Without some level of organizing, there will be chaos. In businesses with more employees there will be more different ideas, more different ways of doing things and more different habits of the people. Organizing is a task that will make all organizational differentiations to work as one whole – the business.

7. Staffing

Staffing is another managerial function. More and more these tasks become important for managers. Selecting the right staff for the business is the heart of the business functioning in the future. Better staff will mean greater business potential energy in the business.

8. Controlling

Controlling is a managerial function like planning, motivating, organizing and staffing. This task is something that will give him the picture for possible errors between planning and actual realization. The goal is to minimize the deviation between something that will like to be and something that becomes the reality.

9. Negotiating

Another important managerial task is negotiating. There are internal and external negotiating. Internal negotiating is negotiating with the entities from inside the businesses. External negotiating is negotiating between managers and external entities that are outside of businesses as suppliers, customers and community. The better negotiating skills of managers will increase overall business potential energy of the business.

10. Delegating

Successful managers know to delegate the right tasks to the right employees. We cannot find the perfect manager. Delegating the tasks to the lower levels is something that differentiates successful managers from average managers. This delegating can combine different knowledge and experience that will bring better accomplishment of the tasks.

11. Representing

The last but not the less important task of managers is representing tasks. The managers are representative of business that they manage. How they look, how they talk, how they walk and how they think will build the picture of the business in the eyes of the people from outside the businesses.

The Art Of Delegating

In today's busy world, one of the best ways to get more time for those top-priority projects is by delegating some of the lower-priority work to someone else. Do any of these reasons sound familiar?

- nobody can do this work as well as I can
- if I delegate this work, there's no guarantee that it'll get done properly
- if someone else does this better than I do, I'm in trouble
- but I haven't got time to teach someone else how to do it
- but I want to be seen as a nice guy, not a slave driver

YOU'RE PART OF A TEAM

Different jobs are performed by different members, and there are various levels of authority and responsibility.
Think of yourself as a member of a team and you'll have a lot less trouble with the concept of delegating.

Here are some tips about how to approach the business of delegating that will save your time and get you the help you need:

- ask for help, don't demand it
- make sure the person has a clear picture of the purpose of any delegated work and knows what kind of results you expect.
- take the time to talk it through, explaining specifically what you're looking for
- encourage questions
- give the person all the information and other resources they'll need to complete the project
- set a realistic deadline that's agreeable and workable for both of you
- keep yourself available for questions, and when necessary ask for periodic progress reports

- don't assume a person will be able to complete a delegated task without any additional help or assistance from you
- never give a person a task you yourself aren't familiar with. (and, don't toss a pile of papers on somebody's desk at 5 P.M. and say, "I want this done by tomorrow morning."...it can be grounds for a revolt)
- give the person the opportunity to be imaginative and take the initiative.
- if you feel the job is being done poorly or incorrectly, pitch in and help.
- take the time to teach the person how to do it the correct way.
- when the project has been completed, give lots of praise and credit for a job well done.

KEEP TRACK OF DELEGATED WORK

Delegating a job to someone else doesn't mean you can forget about it. Put the person's initials next to the item on your things to-do list and enter the deadline you've both agreed upon on your calendar.

Don't cross that job off your list until it's been successfully completed.

If you're delegating a part of a larger project, you need to make doubly sure that the work is completed on time; otherwise the whole project may be delayed.

Delegating is a confidence builder, for both the delegate and the delegator. With practice you'll gain confidence in your own ability to delegate and in your colleague's ability to complete the work.

Your colleagues will become more sure of their ability to handle the job. And you will both feel the satisfaction of making an important contribution to your team - and to the success of your company.

The ability to delegate effectively has a double payoff. You'll save time, which you can spend on other important projects, and you'll send a signal to your colleagues and superiors that you're an effective manager of your time and an excellent team player - maybe even captain material.

Delegation done right can be very rewarding and you're the ultimate winner.

The 12 Rules of Delegation

Delegation is one of the most important skills. Technical professionals, team and business leaders, managers, and executives all need to develop good delegation skills. There are many rules and techniques that help people to delegate. Good delegation saves money, time, builds people and team skills, grooms successors and motivates people. Poor delegation sucks! Ask any employee. It causes frustration, demotivates and confuses people and teams. It is important to develop good delegation skills. These twelve rules of delegation should help you out.

1. Delegation is a two-way street. That's right! Delegation is meant to develop you and the people you work with. Consider what you are delegating and why you are delegating it. Are you delegating to build people, get rid of work you don't like to do or to develop someone?

2. To be a good delegator you need to let go. You can't control everything so let go and trust the people you work with. Hand over those tasks to other people that are stopping you from reaching your full potential.

3. Create a delegation plan. Use a delegation matrix that shows your people and the main task components and how you can develop your people and get the work done. This will help your people understand the expectations being set.

4. Define the tasks that must be done. Make sure that the task can be delegated and is suitable to be delegated. Some things you have to do and others can be done by someone else. Be clear on what the task is and is not. People like clarity when being delegated to. So ensure you are clear. If you are not clear your people will not be and you will be disappointed. Worst, your people will feel like failures. Not cool!

5. Select and assign the individual or team that should take on the task. Be clear on your reasons for delegating the task to that person or team. Be honest with yourself. Make sure you answer the question what are they going to get out of it and what you are going to get out of it? Think of it as listening to the radio station WII-FM (what's in it for them). It's a good motivator.

6. Make sure you consider ability and training needs. The importance of the task may need to be defined. Can the people or team do the task? Do they understand what needs to be done? If not, you can't delegate it to them. If resources are an issue, sit your team down and move things around or develop a mentoring-support program that enables your people.

7. Clearly explain the reason for the task or work that must be done. Discuss why the job is being delegated and how it fits into the scheme of things. Don't be afraid to negotiate points that are discussed when appropriate. Don't say it is because we are told to do it. For your people to own the task you must own the task. Reframe and rephrase it so you have ownership.

8. State the required outcomes and results. Answer questions like what must be achieved, what the measurements will be, and clarify how you intend to decide that the job was successfully done.

9. Be prepared to discuss the required resources with the individual and team. Common challenges arise with every person and team including people, location, time, equipment, materials and money. These are important concerns and should be discussed and solved creatively. However, sometimes it is simply as it must be done. Be prepared.

10. Get agreement on timeline and deadlines. Include a status reporting feature to ensure things are getting done. When is the job to be done? What are the ongoing operational duties? What is the status report date and how is it due? Make sure you confirm an understanding of all the previous items. Ask for a summary in their words. Look for reassurance that the task can be done. Address any gaps and reinforce your belief in the individuals or teams work. They need to know you trust them.

11. Remember the two way street, well it is most likely a multi-directional intersection. Look around and support and communicate. Speak to those people who need to know what is going on. Check your stakeholders list and make sure you inform them what the individuals or teams responsibility is. Do not leave it up to the individual or team. Keep politics, the task profile and importance in mind.

12. Provide and get feedback for teams members and individuals. It is important that you let people know how they are doing and if they are achieving their aim. Don't get into blame-storming. You must absorb the consequences of failure, create an environment where failure is an opportunity to learn and grow and pass on the credit for success. Pay it forward if you can.

Delegation used as a tool develops you and your people. The better you are at delegation the better the people around you and your teams will do. It is part of command skills and should be used to let go and trust in your people. The difference between success and failure is often a matter of letting go and delegating.

Time Management Expert

One day an expert in time management was speaking to a group of business students and, to drive home a point, used an illustration those students will never forget. As he stood in front of the group of high-powered overachievers he said, "Okay, time for a quiz."

Then he pulled out a one-gallon, wide mouth Mason jar and set it on the table in front of him. Then he produced about a dozen fist-sized rocks and carefully placed them, one at a time, into the jar. When the jar was filled to the top and no more rocks would fit inside, he asked, "Is this jar full?"

Everyone in the class said, "Yes."

Then he said, "Really?" He reached under the table and pulled out a bucket of gravel. Then he dumped some gravel in and shook the jar causing pieces of gravel to work themselves down into the space between the big rocks.

Then he asked the group once more, "Is the jar full?"

By this time the class was on to him. "Probably not," one of them answered.

"Good!" he replied. He reached under the table and brought out a bucket of sand. He started dumping the sand in the jar and it went into all of the spaces left between the rocks and the gravel. Once more he asked the question, "Is this jar full?"

"No!" the class shouted.

Once again he said, "Good." Then he grabbed a pitcher of water and began to pour it in until the jar was filled to the brim.

Then he looked at the class and asked, "What is the point of this illustration?"

One eager beaver raised his hand and said, "The point is, no matter how full your schedule is, if you try really hard you can always fit some more things in it!"

"No," the speaker replied, "that's not the point. The truth this illustration teaches us is: If you don't put the big rocks in first, you'll never get them in at all."

What are the "big rocks" in your life? Time with your loved ones? Your faith, your education, your dreams? A worthy cause? Teaching or mentoring others?

Remember to put these BIG ROCKS in first or you'll never get them in at all.

Source Unknown

Successful People Increase the Value of Their Time...

Successful people put a high value on their time. They don't waste it. They realize that time is the most valuable asset they have, so they do everything they can to get maximum results.

If you want to get ahead in life, you can't afford to waste time. You've got to get the most out of each day. You've got to complete your work, tasks, and projects on time, do them well, and do them right. In this article you'll discover many of time-saving tips, techniques, ideas, and strategies that will help you get more out of each day.

Anecdote: It's the only game we're playing.

Before every game, just after the national anthem was played, someone on a Major League team would yell: "Hey, this is a really big game, guys." "Why's that?" someone else would ask. "Because it's the only one we're playing," a third person would shout. During the months that ritual was followed, the team had the best won-lost record in the league. And so it is with life. This isn't a practice session. There isn't another "game" after this one. This is it. Life it as if it's the only one you'll ever have...because it is.

Increase the Value of Your Time

We've all heard the phrase "Time is money." But what does that really mean? It means that the things you know-your skills, talents, knowledge, and experience-have value and that someone is willing to pay you for them. So when you're not fully utilizing your God-given skills, talents, knowledge, and experience, you are indeed wasting money.

Ask yourself: "How much value do I put on my time?

Remember:

Your skills, talents, knowledge, and experience are the most valuable assets you've got. Success Tip:
MAKE THE MOST OF YOUR GIVEN TALENTS, AND YOU'LL BE COMPENSATED BEYOND YOUR WILDEST DREAMS.

The greater the value you put on your time, your skills, and your talents, the more you're going to accomplish, because you will utilize them better. You'll reach your goals and achieve your dreams sooner. And when those goals have been reached, you'll set your sights on even bigger ones.

Give Yourself A Raise.

Put a higher value on your time and you'll spend it differently. Learn how to use your time more effectively and you'll accomplish a lot more and make a lot more money.
In order to accomplish more in your life, you've got to perform at a higher level. Yes, there are only 24 hours in a day, and you spend somewhere between 8 and 10 of them working. (And if you add commuting time, you've probably got a 10-, 12-, or even 14-hour day.)

So we're not going to ask you to put in any more hours. We just want to ask you a question: "How do you spend those 8 to 10 working hours?" Here's how to improve the way you spend your time so that you'll accomplish much more every day, and in the end have more time for your family, your friends, and yourself.

Just for the fun, pretend that someone is willing to pay you $600 an hour for your skills, talents, knowledge, and experience. Multiply that out. Eight hours a day is $4800. Five days a week is $24,000. And 50 weeks a year (you do get a vacation) is $1,200,000. Now we're talking real money.

And, since we're sure you work 10, or even 12 hours a day, and probably Saturdays and parts of Sundays, these figures are on the light side. But the goal isn't to put in more hours. It's to get more out of the hours you do work.

$600 an hour conveniently works out to $10 a minute. So, to take a $10 bill out of your purse or wallet, put it on the table, and look at it for a minute. At $10 a minute you can see time. At $10 a minute your colleagues and co-workers can see time. At $10 a minute, you won't waste time.

You won't waste your valuable time sitting on hold for several minutes while you're waiting for someone to get off the telephone. You'll leave a message or call back later.

You won't waste 15 to 30 minutes of your valuable time sitting in a reception area as you wait for the person with whom you've scheduled a meeting to complete his/her current meeting. Instead, you'll make it a point to confirm all your meetings and appointments before you leave your office so you can adjust your schedule if others are running a bit late.

And, speaking of meetings, you'll insist that they start on time, end on time, and accomplish the things they were supposed to accomplish. At $10 per minute, multiplied by everybody in the meeting, you just can't afford to waste time. It's just too expensive.

Once you begin to realize your time is worth this kind of money, you'll start spending it differently. You'll do only the things that are really important. You'll eliminate the things that keep you busy and waste your time. You'll focus your time and energies on the tasks you must accomplish so that you'll achieve your goals.

Success Tip:

The decisions that come out of meetings can be worth tens of thousands or tens of millions of dollars to your company. They can affect your raises, bonuses, and promotional opportunities. The benefits of a well-run meeting can greatly exceed the cost of $10 per minute for those in attendance.

Remember:

The way you spend your time is a result of the way you see your time and the way you see your priorities.

Remember:

Give yourself a raise - in your mind - increase your level of performance, and you'll travel much faster down the road to success. You'll also make more money than you ever dreamed.

Now, take a moment to think about how you spend your 8 to 10 hours during the workday. What are your five biggest time-wasters? How much time is wasted on each of them every day? What can you do to eliminate or reduce this drain on your time, energy, and enthusiasm?

Give Yourself an Extra Hour Each Day

As a young man I discovered this concept, quite by accident. Living with my grandparents during the summer at an idyllic lake, I rarely go out of bed before mid-morning...since most of my friends at the lake slept in. One morning I woke up very early...about 4:30 in the morning. I got dressed and wandered down to the lakeshore. The surface of the lake was like a mirror. Schools of perch flashed bright silver in the early morning sun, just below the surface. A solitary loon was still paddling around, occasionally diving for food. No cars. No boats, Nobody. Just nature...and me. It was wonderful, at sixteen; to have made this discovery...that there was seemingly 'another world' of wonder, beauty, and opportunity...just waiting to be experienced. From that morning on, I promised myself never to waste my time in this world by not making the time for what I really wanted to do.

Over the years, I've taken this concept to heart. When I've wanted to complete something that was very important to me, I would get up at 5:00 A.M. and work for an hour or longer before eating breakfast.
When you have work that is very important to you, get up early and give yourself an extra hour of uninterrupted time each day. You're bright and alert, you have lots of energy, your concentration level is high and most importantly, you're highly motivated. You'll be amazed at how much you're able to accomplish when you focus your energies on completing a single task. As well, you'll be amazed, as I was, all those years ago, with what I experienced.

Time-Saving Tip:

Many of us spend several hours a day commuting to and from work. If you're one of them, would it be possible to change your schedule so as to avoid the heavy traffic? This would enable you to convert commuting time-to-time you can use more productively and effectively. To go one step further...perhaps you can change your work schedule so you could work from home one or two days a week and eliminate the commute altogether.

Do One More Thing Before You Call it a Day

At the end of each day, look at your daily to-do list and do one more task before you call it a day. Make one more phone call. Write one more letter. Find one more thing you can accomplish and cross off your list before you go home.

Anecdote:

The concept of making one more phone call or completing one more task before calling it a day has helped me further my career in many ways. Since I started doing this I've reached hundreds of people who were still sitting at their desks at 5:30 P.M. The "gatekeeper" had gone home...so there was no one to screen their calls. And I've completed thousands of tasks that have enabled me to stay a couple of steps ahead of my competition.

Think of the impact this will make for you. At the end of your week, you'll have completed five more items that were on your to-do list. At the end of the month, an additional 20 items will have been completed. And at the end of the year you'll have completed an extra 200 tasks.

Remember:

Get more things done during the course of the day, and you'll have more time to chart your course...which means you can really accomplish your goals...the ones you've only dreamed of achieving.

Time-Saving Tip:

Don't put off till tomorrow what can be done today...because tomorrow may never come...right?

Super Quick Time Study

In order to grow your business, you will need to carve 10 to 20 hour a week out of your busy schedule. Considering that you are probably working 60 to 80 hours, this may be difficult but should not be impossible. Once you have some time to invest in team building and marketing, you will see your business begin to grow. Let's find out where your time is going...

1. Fill in the chart below to estimate how much time you spend per each day of the typical week working in your business:

Day of week	Hours
Total	

2. Fill in the chart below with the 5 to 10 tasks categories you do on a weekly basis. E.g. communication (mail, phone, email), delivery of products, bookkeeping, sales calls, meeting with clients, production time in plant, working front desk, etc.

Task	Hours
Total	

3. Re-work and re-figure the numbers in these tables until the Total Hours in both tables are approximately equal. This will give you a good picture of what tasks are consuming your time.

4. Now, choose the one or two task categories that can be delegated. Your coach will work with you to develop a plan to delegate one or two areas to other team members in your business or to a new recruit to your business. If you need to hire a team member, see our FOUR HOUR FORMAT HIRING SYSTEM.

Keys to Time Management

BASIC PREMISES:

1. Accept – you will never be able to do everything you want… because there is just too much to do.

2. The driving force (purpose) behind managing your time is to accomplish your ultimate goal/s.

FOUR SKILLS TO USE YOUR TIME WISELY REQUIRE:

- Analysis
- Planning
- Delegation
- Self-management

The Process for Success:

What to do:

- Spend your time doing what is key to the success of your business.
- Work on tasks that can only be done effectively by you. (4 "D's" -- Do it…. Delegate it….Defer it….or Dump it)

When to do:

Plan your time/ organize your work schedule so that you are never working the issues that fall into the "important/urgent" category.

How to do (organize): Tool – Time blocking chart

Create a "template" schedule for each time period – month/week/day - which allocates time periods for specific types of tasks. Ex: travel to customers, return/place phone calls; do quiet work, organize paperwork, read.

How to do (discipline): Tool – Daily, Weekly lists

Work off of lists & mark the items for priority (a,b,c) - the key to efficient use of time is planning.

PLANNING:

How to Generate More Clients Profitably

- Gather your materials in advance, so can "hit the ground running"

For motivation

- Put as much on your list as you can, momentum gained as you check off
- When large projects, break them into small steps so you can see progress.

For effectiveness

• Each major project should be planned out over time periods with other activities interspersed.

HINTS FOR SUCCESS:

• Incremental progress is key. So for projects, "divide to multiply". Start now, step by step.

• Do the toughest things first –

- Stops procrastination

- You'll feel great... therefore...

- You'll be inspired to do everything else required for the day

- Delegate: Include scheduled time in your plan to oversee/ train/ obtain & review reports on the work you have delegated. Do not slip into the habit of doing it.

IF YOU SCHEDULE ON IMPORTANCE, NOT URGENCY – THE URGENT WILL ALMOST NEVER OCCUR!

www.moreprofitlesstime.com | www.ceo-ondemand.com

Email and SMS etiquette

The rules of email SMS etiquette are not "rules" in the sense that I will come after you if you don't follow them. They are guidelines that help avoid mistakes (like offending someone when you don't mean to) and misunderstandings (like being offended when you're not meant to). These core rules of email and SMS etiquette help us communicate better via email and SMS.

1. Take Another Look Before You Send a Message
Don't send anything you don't want to send.

2. Do Not Default to "Reply All"
"Reply" is good. "Reply to All" is better. Right?

3. Keep Emails Short
Do not intimidate recipients with too much text.

4. Properly Format Your Email Replies, and Be Lazy
Do you think quoting original text in your email replies perfectly is a lot of work? Don't let the '>' intimidate you! Here's a very comfortable, relaxed, quick and still clean and compatible way to reply properly.

5. Write Perfect Subject Lines
Do you make these mistakes in your email subjects? (The key to getting your messages read is not to be clever.)

6. Clean Up Emails Before Forwarding Them
Forwarding emails is a great way of sharing ideas, but make sure the original idea is not hidden in obfuscation.

7. When in Doubt, Send Plain Text Email, Not Rich HTML
Not everybody can receive your fancily formatted emails. Some may even react furious. To be safe rather than sorry, send plain text emails only when in doubt.

8.   Don't Forward Hoaxes

Email hoaxes often contain stories that are intriguing, and sure to irritate. Here's how to spot and stop urban legends.

9.   Use Antivirus Software, Keep Up to Date, Scan for Free

Make sure you're not spreading worms and viruses via email or act as a vehicle for spreading spam. All this can be caused by malicious emails. Fortunately, there's protection.

10. Explain Why You Think What You Forward Will Interest the Recipient

More and better communication makes better relationships. Here's a way to spot and share relevant information and foster ties by forwarding emails and links.

11. Do Let People Know Their Mail Has Been Received

Did the spam filter eat my message? Spare others this nagging question and let them know you got their email.

12. Ask Before You Send Huge Attachments

Don't clog email systems without permission.

13. Talk About One Subject per Email Message Only

Help make the world less confusing. Try to talk about one subject per message only. For another subject, start a new email.

14. Punctuation Matters; in Emails Too

Comma, colon, hyphen and semicolon — all exist for a reason: they make it easier to understand the intended meaning of a sentence. Don't make life more difficult and possibly less interesting for the recipients of your emails. Pay some — though not too pedantically much — attention to punctuation.

15. Use Acronyms Sparingly -

DYK? Not everybody knows every acronym, and they don't save that much time anyway.

16. Resize Pictures to Handy Proportions for Emails

When your photos look good in your email, you look good, too! Here's how to make sure your images are not larger than screens and mailboxes by resizing them in style — online and for free.

17. Writing in All Caps is Like Shouting

Don't shout in your emails (and all caps is so difficult to read).

18. Be Careful with Irony in Emails

No, really! I mean it. Honestly!

19. Catch Typos by Printing Your Emails

You can often find typos or misplaced commas neither your spelling checker nor you yourself catch when proofreading on the screen.

20. Avoid Embarrassing Emails

Avoid embarrassing emails by sending them to yourself only (by default).

21. Set Your System Clock Right

Make sure you don't send messages from 1981.

22. In Doubt, End Emails with "Thanks"

If you don't know how to say good-bye at the end of an email, there's one thing that will almost always be appropriate. Thanks.

23. Where to Put Your Signature

Without a line sub-scripted "sign here", how do you decide where to place your email signature? Look here.

24. Wondering "How to Put That in Writing", Write "That"

Tell it like it is. Have you notices how people who you understand perfectly well when you listen to them become cryptic when they start writing?

25. Compress Files Before Sending Them via Email

Smaller is more beautiful, at least when it comes to email attachments. So make files smaller before your send them via email.

26. Avoid "Me Too" Messages

"Me too" is not enough content, but too much annoyance.

Business Essentials Series...

Disc 1 in the Business Essentials Series
Gaining Focus in Your Business

This is about your fundamental learning skills and what you will need to do to change them to vastly improve the way you look
at your development to become a truly effective business owner not just simply remain self-employed.

You will also give you some excellent tools to set goals, work on your plans and create a diary that will allow you to steal your time back to begin moving your business from chaos to control.

Disc 2 in the Business Essentials Series
Getting Your Financials Right

You will learn the importance of understanding your financials.

After all being in business is about making profit and having cash flow work for YOU since you are responsible for your profits.
Become your accountant and book keepers best friend by understanding more about how the financials in your business works so you can ask them better questions to maximise your profits not simply ensure tax compliance.

Disc 3 in the Business Essentials Series
Leveraging Your Business Harder

You will learn the principles of what and how to leverage far more in your business to get more from less and to work far smarter and not just harder.

Here is where you will receive some of the tools you will need to better understand how to get your business flying, what it is you need to test and measure, how to do it and WHY it's so important.

Disc 4 in the Business Essentials Series
How to Generate More Clients Profitably

This is where you will determine your uniqueness, develop a meaningful guarantee and learn the basics of good advertising.

You will gain a better appreciation between the difference of Marketing and Advertising, learn how to get the most for the least investment and ensure that you do it all profitably.

Disc 5 in the Business Essentials Series
Maximising Your Conversion Rates

Get to know how your Sales Pipeline REALLY works and how to identify who your suspects really are, convert prospects into regular shoppers and understand how much more work you can do to maximise your sales experience.

Disc 6 in the Business Essentials Series
Meet and Exceed Your Clients Expectations

Now you have new customers, how do you make sure you KEEP them, how do you wanting to come back time and again while telling their friends? ...this is where you really make a difference.

Disc 7 in the Business Essentials Series
Systemising Your Business For Consistent Excellence

Do you recognise the importance of having systems in your business and how they can improve your profitability? We show you how to systemise like a corporate while retaining the culture of a smaller business. Understanding how we systemise for routine and humanise for the exceptions will enable you to be the best in your field every time.

Disc 8 in the Business Essentials Series
Do You Have a Champion Team with a Champion Leader?
This is about having the right people on the bus. It starts with you however so you'll learn how to maximise your own skills and then you will attract and retain the right people.

When you understand how the TEAM is the most important part of your business and what needs to be done to achieve the very best from yourselves and others you are well on your way to becoming a better manager of this invaluable resource.

Disc 9 in the Business Essentials Series
The Essentials of Getting Your Time Back.
This is where you get to redefine your time management You will understand better how you can start working far more on the business than in the business than ever before.

You will also finally find out why others can seem to fit more into their day while having a great LIFE – WORK balance (notice the order!)..

Disc 10 in the Business Essentials Series
Simply Brilliant Customer Service.
It's so easy to give mediocre or good customer service but it's just as easy to give amazing service to your customers and delight them.

You will understand the simple easy steps that you must take to provide consistently brilliant service and how to get your team excited about doing it.

Disc 11 in the Business Essentials Series
Discovering DISC and EQ not just IQ.
We believe for things to change first you must change so here you will learn why you behave as you do and just as importantly understand why other people react and act the way they do.

You will also learn what DISC really is and what it isn't. You will learn how to apply these important principles in your recruitment and team management / development.

You will learn how to use these ideas in creating a more dynamic team and discover the what and why of emotional intelligence. You will also develop key strategies for using the knowledge here and the tools we have available on our website and why we place such a massive emphasis on DISC and other tools that support, train and develop your team.

You will also learn how to use these skills and observations at home and socially not just at the workplace.

Disc 12 in the Business Essentials Series
Quality Recruitment.
Recruitment of the right people for the right reasons in the right roles for your team is so incredibly important yet so often ignored or pushed to the rear.

You will learn who the right person is for your business and the role you want filled.
You will be able to identify the right people early in the process to save yourself and them the time and money wasted with antique recruitment methodologies that just don't work anymore.

How to get the best out of your recruitment activities so you can keep the assets you acquire for the long term and get the best return from your investment.

ABOUT THE AUTHOR

John Millar is the Managing Director, Senior Business Coach Trainer and Consultant with More Profit Less Time Pty Ltd and CEO-ONDEMAND. Along with his many other business interests, John is proud to have been an associate of the most successful coaching team in the world.

He is recognized as a global leader and has been benchmarked against over 1,300 colleagues in 31 countries. John has over 25 years of hands-on ownership, management, coaching, and entrepreneurial experience in a broad range of industry sectors, including retail, wholesale, import, export, IT, trades and trade services, automotive, primary production, food services, transport, manufacturing, mining, professional services, the fitness industry, and more.

He has extensive experience developing and providing training for small to medium-sized companies and a variety of publicly listed corporate companies. John is an accomplished and talented public and professional speaker. He has been a mentor working with sales/management activities for businesses with a turnover under $100,000 per annum, over $100 million turnover, and everything in between, with great success.

John currently works with business owners and their teams across Australia and has a "Whatever it takes" attitude that has enabled him to help his clients grow their business profits by up to 800%.

 If you are ready to be coached by one of the best in the business, register at:

www.ceo-ondemand.com.au

Make sure to visit www.moreprofitlesstime.com for the new online Management Development Program: The Business Essentials Series.

ACCLAIM FOR JOHN MILLAR'S
Business Coaching and Training in their own words...

"Without John Millar as my Business Coach I wouldn't have a business today."—Grant Jennings Managing Director, Jigsaw Projects

"Taking the decision to be coached and trained by John Millar was carefully considered after experiencing those who over promised and under delivered. I am pleased to say the content of his courses are the tools we all need to master as business owners. His delivery is engaging, thought provoking and empowering and after every session l came away re-energised. John always makes himself available for business building advice both via Skype and face to face beyond the scope of delivery. With his extensive personal experience in building small businesses, he knows and understands what it takes to establish and grow a business. I have no hesitation endorsing John Millar as an educator and business coach and the bonus is he is a very nice person."—Anne Lederman Managing Director FB Salons"

Johns training with my management team was excellent, it was very different from the business coaching and support I have had in the past. John was clear, thoughtful and he addressed the issues we needed to cover without us even knowing they were being addressed! His follow up has been fantastic and exactly what I needed. I would recommend John and his team to anyone looking at getting some business coaching and training done" —Wendy Crawford, Peopleworx

"In my dealings with John as our business coach, I have found him to be a motivated and insightful agent of positive change. He is able to burrow down to the root cause of issues and introduce effective forms of measurement. John then identifies and implements practical solutions and is there to provide the gentle persuasion required to ensure that results are achieved." —Mark Felton, Lindale Insurances

"You have coached and trained us so well throughout the year that we are now used to & find it easy to prepare a 90 day plan, then breaks it down to actionable bite size pieces. Planning in business & personal life certainly is important. It allows us to identify the important things & the bigger picture. Thank you for your support & guidance throughout the year. And not to mention your insight, external perspective to review & assist our business moving forward." —Linda Turner, Director Roy A McDonald Certified Practicing Accountants

"If you want to achieve sales results you never thought were possible and give yourself a competitive edge my strong suggestion is to engage John services and listen closely to what John has to say, during the time I was trained by John I was one of eight sales consultants in a national business for 10 out of the 13 months I lead the sales tally and in 1 quarter I generated three times the revenue of the national sales force combined. Johns training and experience was well worth the investment and paid big dividends. Thanks John." —Julian Fadini, Bellvue Capital

"John is a very enthusiastic trainer and business coach, he is very passionate about getting business owners and their team where they need to be. He goes the extra mile to keep ahead of the latest developments which he then uses to benefit his clients." —Darren Reddy CPA

"I have been to a few seminars and heard John speak numerous times about sales, marketing and business. He is a very knowledgeable and extremely enthusiastic business coach in all his interactions and I would recommend him to all business owners who need a sales and marketing boost!" —Andrew Heath, Managing Director, Fresh Living Group

"I worked with John Millar and found his business knowledge, passion and innovation to be inspiring. He has always been able to set (and achieve) strategic long and short-term goals both for himself and his clients without losing that personal connection he builds with everyone he meets. He has been and I believe will continue to be a strong mentor and trainer for anyone wanting to take that next step in their business." —Bree Webster, Online Marketing Guru

"Massive Action Day" – what an understatement, John Millars 4 hour frenzy challenged me to seriously review areas of my business I would not have gone to …. In this way, the process identified incongruence's in my mind, my business and my modus operandi. It's created a paradigm shift. Thanks John, the road map just got a whole lot clearer. Your friendship and insights since 2003 have been a gift to my business and I." —Andrew Reay, Counsellor, Hypnotherapist and Counsellor, Thinkshift Transformations

"John Millar is not your usual Business coach or trainer; he gets involved with you and your business and provides hands on help to make sure you follow through on his advice. He is highly motivated to help his clients and his personal guarantee certainly shows this. He has now transposed his thoughts, advice and love of good business onto a series of DVD's in his business venture – More Profit Less Time. This has excellent tips and advice for anyone either starting out or already in business. I highly recommend John to any business owner who wants to run a business and not a j.o.b.!" —Darren Cassidy, Managing Director HR2U

"I and many of my Business Partners and colleagues have worked with John since 2010 as our business oath, trainer and motivator and found him to be an extremely motivational person to assist us achieve our business goals. This company and its products allows for John's skill set to be accessed by a wider number of potential clients. His very professional DVD series is extremely good value for money and is easily accessible for all of us who are time poor. If you are looking to maximise your and your business's results and to start achieving your goals and dreams, contact John; you won't look back!!" —Mark Cleland, Mortgage Choice

"John develops real relationships with the people he comes into contact with. He is pasionate about what he does. His DVD and group training series, is full of good ideas and process to make your business better. Knowing what to do and actually doing it are two different things. John is excellent at helping you get things done." —Carey Rudd, Sales Director, Online Knowledge

"I have known John since 2004 and found him to be extremely knowledgably in both Sales and Business systems as a business coach without peer. John has provided me with business advice as well as personal coaching over the years, helping me with the running of my organisation. I'm impressed with John's DVD series where he has condensed a lot of the information in an easy to follow format that any business owner can use immediately. I wish he had released these DVDs earlier, as they are a goldmine of information, and practical how to that allow anyone to increase the profit in their business and get back valuable wasted time." —Steve Psaradellis, Managing Director, TEBA

"John's DVD and workbook delivery of his no-nonsense advice provides a low-cost option for those business owners looking to set and achieve goals that will increase profit. I found the conversational style of the DVD's easy to follow, whilst the requirement to pause the DVD and write down some action points ensured a level of commitment to the advice being provided." — Mark Felton, Lindale Insurances

"I only met John briefly at a BNI meeting and knew instantly i need to hire him for my business as my business coach. His attitude towards work and how to improve my cash line had an instant effect on before, even before I finally hired him on an official basis. I found myself thinking "what would John do" and this was only after just meeting him. I cannot see my business expend and give me "More Profit Less Time" without John's expert direction and training. If you want to succeed in business life, you need John Millar, without him you're just kidding yourself " —Leslie Cachia, Managing Director, Letac Drafting

"I can highly recommend John Millar to any business owner who wants to grow his business. When I hear very positive feedback from colleagues who are skeptics by nature about John's ability and skills, I know John will help all those he comes in contact with. John comes with a selfless nature and the willingness to work inside a client's business to make it succeed. Rare indeed!" —Darren Cassidy, Managing Director, HR2U"I first met John Millar in mid-2010 and have always found him to be of an honest and generous character that engenders an easy association with him. I love how easy he is to listen to and how passionate he is about his work and topics. John demonstrates a love for life and his work and I have no hesitation in recommending his services." —Kathie M Thomas, Managing Director, VA

"I have listened to John speak on a number of occasions and find him a very knowledgeable speaker with a passion for what he does. I have also interacted with a number of his clients and they all tell me that he helps them achieve results in their business. If you are looking for business help John is a person you can trust." —Carey Rudd, Sales Director, Online Knowledge

"John knows his stuff, he knows how the get results, John has so many great ideas in building a business and helping business owners work less and make more money. John has released a DVD set on doing just that. I have watched the 1st one and it was great, very informative and easy to understand, I happily recommend John to anyone in need of help and guidance" —Frank Eramo, Proprietor, Dynotune

"I have known John only for a short time, however the impact that he has had on me, not just my business has helped me to visualise opportunities that I began to doubt my ability to realise. He is encouraging and at the same time challenging so that he can/you can, begin to see how to maximise the business potential, John calls it being an unreasonable friend, I call it being a mate. If you have any questions about the direction of your business, if you want to seem your bottom line improve not just turnover but real profit, if you want a person who will work with you then I strongly recommend that you engage him at your earliest convenience. John is the best thing that has happened to my business. I could tell you about the way he is on track to make 1/2 a million for me on his contacts alone, but that actually sells him short, he has become like my partner in business, and cares about my success as if it was his own, we will flourish because I took the step to employ his training to help me grow. If you get a chance to get him training you, don't wait like I did, get in as quickly as possible, his time is your business and if like me your business is to make money, then every day you don't have him on retainer you lose money." —Russell Summers, Managing Director, The Give Life Centre

"It's usually easy to be mediocre in business but it's impossible when you have John Millar training you. He has been my right hand since 2003!" —David Manser, CFO, Hydrosteer

"I now have a commercial, profitable business and now it's my choice when I work IN my business and when I work ON it and have had john helping me in business since 1988. I can't imagine not having John as a part of our business." —David Wall, Director, D&K Transport

"The work John has done since 2008 coaching and training our marketing team, administration and finance teams, buyers, store managers and staff nationally have been fantastic." —Ross Sudano, Director, Anaconda Adventure Stores

"John is a creative, professional, practical and committed business coach and trainer. His approach since we first met him in 1994 to working with a client team through the application of useful tools, information and anecdotes along with his easy going & easy to understand delivery sets him apart from other business coaches that I have used in the past." —Anthony Beasley, Director, The Astra Group

"I have worked with John Millar for the since 2004 and I didn't think it was possible to achieve what we have achieved together. His business coaching, training and services just get better and better!" —Terrance Chong, Managing Director, Echo Graphics and Printing

"John's business coaching, training and support has transformed our business across Australia and New Zealand since 2008."—Rose Vis, Managing Director, VIP Australia

"We first met John in 2005, he is AMAZING at sales, marketing, operations, logistics, finance training and so much more. Since engaging John as our business coach our business has exploded, our team are happy, our clients are raving about us and my husband and I now take at least 12 weeks holidays a year, EVERY year." —Shirley Du, Director, Goldline Technology

"It's the no nonsense results driven business coaching and training focus John bought to the table that had such a massive effect on our business." —David Runkel, Director, Tracomp Fabrication and Steel

"We started working with John in early 2010, within 90 days of working with and being trained by John Millar we had the biggest and most profitable month in our 15 year history. That's impressive." —Hugh Gilchrist, Managing Director, Australian Moulding Company

"If you don't have John as your business trainer you aren't meeting your business potential." — Don Robertson, Director, Medallion Electrical Services

Thank You